Wisdom of the West

a historical survey of Western Philosophy in its social and political setting

Wisdom of the West

Bertrand Russell

editor **Paul Foulkes**

designer Edward Wright   with ten Compositions by John Piper

Crescent Books, Inc.

ISBN 0-517-06420-0
Library of Congress Catalog Card No. 59-11326
© MCMLIX Rathbone Books Limited, London
Printed and bound in Yugoslavia by Mladinska Knjiga, Ljubljana
Reprinted 1977 and 1978